DISCOVER
THE ART OF
Vegetarian
Chinese

**CHEF
DHARMENDRA
SHARMA**

BlueRose ONE
Stories Matter
New Delhi • London

BLUEROSE PUBLISHERS
India | U.K.

Copyright © Chef Dharmendra Sharma 2024

All rights reserved by author. No part of this publication may be reproduced, stored in a retrieval system or transmitted in any form or by any means, electronic, mechanical, photocopying, recording or otherwise, without the prior permission of the author. Although every precaution has been taken to verify the accuracy of the information contained herein, the publisher assume no responsibility for any errors or omissions. No liability is assumed for damages that may result from the use of information contained within.

BlueRose Publishers takes no responsibility for any damages, losses, or liabilities that may arise from the use or misuse of the information, products, or services provided in this publication.

For permissions requests or inquiries regarding this publication,
please contact:

BLUEROSE PUBLISHERS
www.BlueRoseONE.com
info@bluerosepublishers.com
+91 8882 898 898
+4407342408967

ISBN: 978-93-6452-236-6

Cover design: Daksh
Typesetting: Tanya Raj Upadhyay

First Edition: September 2024

Chef Dharmendra Sharma

Not everyone who cooks is a chef. It takes lot of determination & humanism.

Undefined trust which was built with this uniform 24 years back when I first wore it...

I explored different cuisines, their versatility and authenticity.

Food is Precedence. Therefore, I devote my life for cooking & making people happy.

I believe Chefs are real life warriors defeating unseen wars every day. Doctors save life for once; chef's save life every day

COOKING IS MY PASSION, UNIFORM IS MY PRIDE

▶ CHEF DHARMENDRA SHARMA
ASSOCIATE DIRECTOR FOOD PRODUCTION

TABLE OF CONTENTS

STARTER 1
   STUFFED EGGPLANT IN BLACK BEAN SAUCE 3
   STIR FRIED FRENCH BEANS 7
   SPICY CHILLI BEAN CAULIFLOWER 9
   SESAME TOAST 11
   SHANGHAI GIMIKAND 13
   SALT 'N' PEPPER RAW BANANA 17
   KUNG-PAO-OKRA 19
   HUNAN STYLE PANEER 21
   HOT GARLIC SOYA CHAAP 23
   GOLDEN FRIED BABY CORN 25
   CHILLI BASIL MUSHROOM 27
   CRISPY SPICY ARBI (COLOCASSIA) 29
   CRISPY PALAK 33
   CRISPY HONEY CHILLI LOTUS STEM 35
   SZECHUAN CORN DUMPLINGS 39
   CHILLI JACKFRUIT 43

SOUP 45
   VEGETABLE MANCHOW SOUP 47
   LEMON CORIANDER SOUP 49
   HOT 'N' SOUR SOUP 51
   GARLIC AND SPRING ONION SOUP 53

SALAD 55
- KIMCHI SALAD 57
- RAW PAPAYA SALAD 59
- CHINESE PICKLE 61

MAIN COURSE 63
- TOFU IN GINGER SAUCE 65
- MUSHROOM IN HOT CHILLI SAUCE 67
- SZECHUAN PANEER 69
- PINEAPPLE IN SPICY SOYA SAUCE 71
- THREE TREASURES VEGETABLES WITH TOFU 75
- CHILLI BASIL CAULIFLOWER 77
- BABY CORN IN BLACK PEPPER SAUCE 79
- KACHALU IN TIRYAKI SAUCE 81
- CHINESE GREEN IN NOODLE NEST 83
- ZUCCHINI IN ONION GINGER SAUCE 87
- EGGPLANT IN OYSTER SAUCE 89
- POTATO IN HOT GARLIC SAUCE 91
- EXOTIC VEGETABLE IN GARLIC SAUCE 93
- SOYA CHAAP IN BLACK BEAN SAUCE 95
- VEGETABLE BALL IN MANCHURIAN GRAVY 97
- VEGETABLE CHOPSUEY 101

NOODLE 103
- VEGETABLE HAKKA NOODLE 105
- CHILLI GARLIC NOODLE 107
- SHANGHAI NOODLE 109
- SINGAPORIAN NOODLE 111

RICE 113
   VEGETABLE FRIED RICE 115
   PINEAPPLE FRIED RICE 117
   CORN FRIED RICE 119
   BURNT GARLIC RICE 121

DESSERT 123
   DATE PAN CAKE 125
   FRUIT ROLL 127
   HONEY FRIED NOODLE 129
   FRIED ICE CREAM 131

STARTER

STUFFED EGGPLANT IN BLACK BEAN SAUCE

For the Stuffed Eggplant

Ingredients   Quantity produced: 1 portio

- Long Eggplants, sliced   ;   1 medium
- Tofu grated   ;   100gm
- Thai red chilli chopped   ;   ½ tsp.
- Green chilli chopped   ;   ½ tsp.
- Coriander root chopped   ;   ½ tsp.
- Shitake mushroom chopped   ;   1 tbsp.
- Salt   ;   to taste
- To coat   ;   Corn flour
- To cook   ;   Refined flour

For the Black Bean Sauce

- Garlic chopped   ;   4-5 clove
- Ginger chopped   ;   ½ inch
- Green chilli chopped   ;   ½ tsp.
- Thai red chilli chopped   ;   ½ tsp.
- Black bean paste   ;   2 tbsp.
- Chilli paste   ;   ½ tbsp.
- Aromat powder   ;   ½ tsp.
- White pepper powder   ;   ½ tsp.
- Dark soya sauce   ;   1 tbsp.
- Coriander chopped   ;   For garnish
- Spring onion chopped   ;   For garnish

METHOD:-

Slice eggplants into ¾-inch thick. Split in half horizontally without cutting all the way through..

In a mixing bowl, add tofu with the remaining ingredients for the stuffed eggplant. Stuff each eggplant slice.

Coat the eggplant piece in batter of corn flour and refined flour.

Heat the oil. Fry eggplant until golden. Remove the fried eggplant from the pan and set aside.

Take a wok for make the black bean sauce put oil. Once the oil is hot, add garlic, ginger, Thai red chilli, green chilli sauté well.

Then add the water and simmer for a couple minutes then add black bean paste, chilli paste, salt, aromat powder and white pepper powder and dark soya sauce add fried eggplant and finish with coriander and spring onion to let flavours combine. Turn off the heat.

Arrange stuffed eggplants on a serving plate, serve piping hot

STIR FRIED FRENCH BEANS

Ingredients: Quantity produced: 1portion

- French beans boiled   ;   200grm
- Garlic chopped   ;   ½ tbsp.
- Thai red chilli chopped   ;   1 tbsp.
- Salt   ;   to taste
- Aromat powder   ;   ½ tsp.
- White pepper powder   ;   a pinch

METHOD;-

In pan heat oil, adds Garlic and Thai red chilli sauté well. Add salt, aromat powder and white pepper powder stir fry for a minute. Serve hot

SPICY CHILLI BEAN CAULIFLOWER

Ingredients: Quantity produced: 1portion

- Cauliflower par boiled   ;   200 grams
- Garlic chopped   ;   4-5 cloves
- Ginger chopped   ;   ½ inch
- Onion chopped   ;   2 tbsp.
- Red Thai chilli   ;   2-3
- Red chilli paste   ;   ½ tsp.
- Tomato ketchup   ;   2 tbsp.
- Spring onion chopped   ;   3 strips
- White pepper powder   ;   ½ tsp.
- Corn flour   ;   Enough to coat Gobi
- Aromat powder   ;   ½ tsp.
- Oil   ;   For deep frying
- Salt   ;   To taste
- Coriander chopped   ;   For garnish
- Chilli bean paste   ;   2 tbsp.

METHOD:-

In a mixing bowl to cauliflower add salt, white pepper powder, chilli paste, aromat powder and mix well. Coat the pieces of cauliflower in the corn flour and deep Fry until turn into nice golden brown colour keep aside.

Heat up a wok and put oil, ginger, garlic and onion. Sauté well
Add chilli bean paste, tomato ketchup, and red chilli paste. Sprinkle salt, aromat powder, white pepper powder, spring onion, coriander, 1cup of water. Mix well; Simmer the flame and cook until sauce becomes medium thick. Add fried cauliflower and chopped spring onions.
Serve piping hot.

SESAME TOAST

Ingredients: Quantity produced: 1 portion

- Mashed potato ; 100 gram
- .Aromat powder ; ½ tsp.
- Green chilli chopped ; 1 tbsp.
- White pepper powder ; ½ tsp.
- Coriander chopped ; 1 tbsp.
- Garlic chopped ; 1 tbsp.
- Spring onion chopped ; 1 tbsp.
- Salt ; To taste
- White bread slices ; 1 no
- Roasted sesame seeds ; As required
- Oil ; For cooking

METHOD

For making filling -In a large bowl, and add the mashed potatoes, aromat powder, green chilli, white pepper powder, coriander, garlic, spring onion and. salt to taste. Mix it until all the ingredients are well combined. Filling is ready.

Make sesame toast-Take bread slices and spread around 2 tablespoons of the filling evenly on the bread. Lightly press with the spoon, so that the filling sticks to the bread easily.

Take a plate, spread the roasted sesame seeds, and dip the bread with the filling on the roasted sesame seeds and press down firmly and cut the bread into triangle.

In a medium-sized frying pan, heat little oil on medium flame and shallow fry the sesame toast for 2-3 minutes until each side turns golden brown and crisp.

Serve hot with tomato ketchup

SHANGHAI GIMIKAND

Ingredients: Quantity produced: 1 portion

- Jimikand ; 200 grams
- Garlic chopped ; 4-5 cloves
- Ginger chopped ; ½ inch
- Green chillies chopped ; 4-5
- Onion chopped ; ½ tbsp.
- Spring finely chopped ; 3 strips
- White pepper powder ; a pinch
- Corn flour ; 2 tbsp.
- Refined flour ; ½ tbsp.
- Soy sauce ; 1 tbsp.
- Aromat powder ; ½ tsp.
- Chilli oil ; 2 tbsp.
- Red Thai chilli ; 2-3
- Chopped celery ; 1 tbsp.
- Red chilli paste ; ½ tsp.
- Vinegar ; ½ tsp.
- Tomato ketchup ; 2 tbsp.
- Oil ; For deep frying
- Salt ; To taste
- Coriander chopped ; For garnish

METHOD:-

Wash and cut jimikand Transfer in the strainer for few minutes to drain out the water fully.

In a mixing bowl add corn flour, Maida, salt, pepper and mix well.

Coat the pieces in the mixture and deep Fry until jimikand pieces turn into nice golden brown colour, Keep aside.

Heat up a wok and put chilli oil, ginger and garlic Sauté well.

Add Chopped onion, celery, Thai chilli along with green chillies.

Sprinkle salt, aromat powder, white pepper powder Cook on medium high flame.

Add tomato ketchup, red chilli paste and 1 cup of water. Mix well.

Simmer the flame and cook until sauce become medium thick.

Add fried jimikand, vinegar and chopped spring onions.

Serve piping hot.

SALT 'N' PEPPER RAW BANANA

INGRIDENTS   Quantity produced: 1portion

- Peeled & cut raw banana   ;   250 gram
- Corn flour   ;   Enough to coat banana
- Salt   ;   1 ½ tsp.
- Garlic chopped   ;   4-5 clove
- Ginger chopped   ;   ½ inch
- Onion chopped   ;   ½ tbsp.
- Celery chopped   ;   ½ tsp.
- Thai red chilli   ;   ½ tsp.
- Red & green capsicum   ;   2 tbsp.
- Aromat powder   ;   ½ tbsp.
- Vinegar   ;   1 tbsp.
- Sesame oil   ;   ½ tsp.
- Spring onions   ;   4-5
- White pepper powder   ;   ½ tsp.

METHOD

In a bowl add banana with salt, white pepper powder & mix.

Then add enough corn flour to coat banana so they re almost fully white and mostly dry Deep fry in hot oil until cooked through and crispy.

In a pan add 2 tbsp. of oil add garlic, ginger onion, chilli, celery, green chilli, Thai red chilli, red & green capsicum and sauté well.

Add salt, aromat powder & white pepper powder and vinegar

Cook until mixture is soft and a little crispy

Add in fried crispy banana and coriander and mix thoroughly.

Serve in a dish and garnish with spring onion

KUNG-PAO-OKRA

INGRIDENTS   Quantity produced: 1 portion

- Cut okra   ; 250 gram
- Cashew nut fried   ; 12 pcs
- Enough to coat   ; Corn flour
- Salt   ; 1 ½ tsp.
- White Pepper powder   ; 1 ½ tsp.
- Garlic chopped   ; 4-5 clove
- Ginger chopped   ; 1 tbsp.
- Onion chopped   ; 1 tbsp
- Celery chopped   ; ½ tsp.
- Thai red chilli   ; ½ tbsp.
- Green chilli chopped   ; ½ tsp.
- Aromat powder   ; ½ tbsp.
- Vinegar   ; ½ tbsp.
- Sesame oil   ; ½ tsp.
- Coriander fresh chopped ; 1 tbsp.
- Spring onions   ; 4-5 strips
- Refined oil   ; 2 tsp.

METHOD

In a bowl add salt, white pepper powder, aromat powder to okra and mix.

Then add in enough corn flour to coat okra so they're almost fully white and mostly dry. Deep fry in hot oil until cooked through and crispy

In a pan add 2 tbsp. of oil add garlic, ginger onion, chilli, celery, green chilli, Thai red chilli and sauté well add some water.

Add salt, aromat powder & white pepper powder, spring onion and coriander.

Cook until mixture is soft then add sesame oil, vinegar

Add in fried crispy okra and cashew nut and mix through

Serve in a dish and garnish with spring onion

HUNAN STYLE PANEER

INGRIDENTS   Quantity produced: 1

- Triangle cut paneer ; 200 gram
- Corn flour ; Enough to coat
- .Chilli paste ; 1tbsp
- Coriander chopped ; 10-12
- .Salt1 ; ½ tsp.
- White Pepper powder ; 1 ½ tsp.
- Garlic chopped ; 4-5 clove
- Ginger chopped ; 1tbsp.
- Ginger, sliced ; ½ inch
- .Thai red & green chilli (diamond cut) ; 1tbsp
- .Oyster sauce ; 1 ½ tbsp.
- .Soya sauce ; 1½ tbsp.
- Aromat powder ; 1½ tbsp.
- Spring onions chopped ; 4-5
- Chilli oil ; ½ tsp.
- Refined oil ; 2tbsp.

METHOD

In a bowl add paneer, aromat powder, soya sauce & mix.

Then add in enough corn flour to coat paneer sc they're almost fully white and mostly dry. Deep fry in hot oil until cooked through and crispy

In a pan add 2 tbsp. of oil add garlic, ginger, ginger slice, green &Thai red chilli, and sauté well add 1 cup of water.

Add salt, aromat powder & white pepper powder, coriander, spring onion & soya sauce. Cook until mixture is soft and a little crispy

Add fried paneer and mix thoroughly.

Serve piping hot and garnish with spring onion

HOT GARLIC SOYA CHAAP

Ingredients: Quantity produced: 1portion

- Soya chaap   :   250 grams
- Red chilli paste   :   1 tsp.
- Aromat powder   :   ½ tsp.
- White pepper powder   :   ½ tsp.
- Corn flour   :   Enough to coat soya chaap
- Garlic chopped   :   4-5 cloves
- Onion chopped   :   1 tbsp
- Green chillies chopped :   1 tbsp.
- Spring onion chopped   :   3 strips
- Soy sauce   :   1 tbsp.
- Red Thai chilli   :   2-3
- Tomato ketchup   :   2 tbsp.
- Sugar   :   1 pinch
- Oil   :   For deep frying
- Salt   :   To taste
- Coriander fresh, chopped : For garnish

METHOD:-

In a bowl add to soya chaap, chilli paste, salt, aromat powder, white pepper powder& mix.

Then add in enough corn flour to coat soya chaap so they're almost fully white and mostly dry. Deep fry in hot oil until cooked through and crispy

In a pan add 2 tbsp. of oil, add garlic, onion, Thai red chilli, and Sauté well.

Add chilli paste, ketchup, salt, aromat powder & white pepper powder and sugar

Cook until mixture is soft and a little crispy

Add in fried crispy soya chaap and fresh coriander and mix through

Serve in a dish and garnish with spring onion.

GOLDEN FRIED BABY CORN

INGRIDENTS   Quantity produced: 1portion

- Baby corn   :   150 gram
- Corn flour   :   1 ½ tbsp.
- Refined flour   :   2 tbsp.
- Salt   :   ½ tsp.
- Baking powder   :   a pinch
- Aromat powder   :   1 tbsp.
- Water   :   As per required
- Oil   :   For deep fry

METHOD

Clean the baby corn and remove the fibre from it if any.

Heat water in a big sauce pan add salt when it starts boiling and then add baby corn to it. Cook for 3-4 minutes. Do not overcook. The baby corn should be firm and half cooked. Remove from water and pat dry them.

In another bowl, add corn flour, refined flour, aromat powder, salt and baking powder one by one.

Mix well using whisk. Gradually add water and make a thick, smooth batter. Taste and adjust the salt.

Heat oil when the oil is hot, dip baby corn one by one in batter, coat it well with batter and add it to the oil. Once the bubble sound reduces and baby corn becomes golden brown in colour, remove from oil. Place it on the plate Serve hot.

CHILLI BASIL MUSHROOM

INGRIDENTS   Quantity produced: 1portion

- Mushroom cut into half   ; 200 gram
- Corn flour   ; Enough to coat mushroom
- Chilli paste   ; 1tbsp.
- Basil leaves   ; 10-12
- Salt1   ; ½ tsp.
- White Pepper powder   ; 1 ½ tsp.
- Garlic chopped   ; 4-5 clove
- Ginger chopped   ; ½ inch
- Thai red & green chilli (diamond cut)   ; 1tbsp.
- Oyster sauce   ; 1 ½ tbsp.
- Soya sauce   ; ½ tbsp.
- Aromat powder   ; ½ tbsp.
- Spring onions   ; 4-5
- Oil   ; for frying

METHOD

In a bowl mix mushroom with chilli paste, white pepper powder and salt.

Then add in enough corn flour to coat mushroom so they're almost fully white and mostly dry. Deep fry in hot oil until cooked through and crispy

In a pan add 2 tbsp. of oil add basil, garlic, ginger, green chilli, Thai red chilli, and sauté well.

Add oyster sauce, soya sauce, salt, aromat powder & white pepper powder

Cook until mixture is soft and a little crispy

Add in fried crispy mushroom and mix thoroughly

Serve in a dish and garnish with spring onion

CRISPY SPICY ARBI (COLOCASSIA)

Ingredients: Quantity produced: 1 portion

- Arbi (colocassia)   ;   250 grams
- Garlic chopped   ;   4-5 cloves
- Ginger chopped   ;   1 tbsp
- Green chillies chopped   ;   4-5
- Onion chopped   ;   1 tbsp
- Spring onion chopped   ;   3 strips
- White pepper powder   ;   ½ tsp.
- Corn flour   ;   Enough to coat Arbi
- Soy sauce   ;   1 tbsp.
- Aromat powder   ;   ½ tsp.
- Red Thai chilli   ;   2-3
- Chopped celery   ;   1 tbsp.
- .Red chilli paste   ;   ½ tsp.
- Tomato ketchup   ;   2 tbsp.
- Oil   ;   For deep frying
- Salt   ;   To taste
- Coriander chopped   ;   For garnish
- Refined oil   ;   1 tbsp.

METHOD:-

Wash and cut Arbi. Transfer in the strainer for few minutes to drain out the water fully.

In a mixing bowl add corn flour, salt, white pepper powder, chilli paste, aromat powder and. Mix well.

Coat the pieces of Arbi in the mixture and deep Fry until turn into nice golden brown colour. Keep aside.

Heat up a wok and put oil, ginger and garlic. Sauté well.

Add Chopped onion, Thai chilli along with green chillies, Add tomato ketchup, red chilli paste. Sprinkle salt, aromat powder, white pepper powder, spring onion, coriander, 1cup of water. Mix well,

Cook on medium high flame.

Simmer the flame and cook until sauce become medium thick.

Add fried Arbi, and chopped spring onions.

Serve piping hot.

CRISPY PALAK

Ingredients: Quantity produced: 1portion

- Spinach cut into strips ; 250 gram
- Garlic chopped ; 1 tbsp.
- Ginger chopped ; 1 tbsp
- .Onion chopped ; 2 tbsp.
- Thai red chilli chopped ; 1 tbsp.
- salt ; To taste
- Aromat powder ; ½ tsp.
- White pepper powder ; ½ tsp.
- .Sesame oil ; 1 tbsp.
- vinegar ; ½ tbsp
- oil ; For frying

METHOD

Heat the oil in a pan Add spinach in to the well heated oil and fry it to be crispy. Keep aside.

Heat up a wok and put oil, ginger and garlic, onion, Thai red chilli,. Sprinkle salt, aromat powder, white pepper powder, 1cup of water. Mix well; add sesame oil and vinegar for flavour add crispy palak & tossed it. Serve hot

CRISPY HONEY CHILLI LOTUS STEM

INGREDIENTS Quantity produced: 1 portion

- Lotus Stem ; 2 no
- Refined flour ; 3 tbsp.
- Corn Flour ; 2 tbsp.
- Salt ; To taste
- Garlic finely chopped ; 2 tbsp.
- Ginger chopped ; 1 tbsp.
- Thai red chilli chopped ; 1-2 pc
- Green chilli chopped ; 1-2 pc
- Celery chopped ; ½ tsp.
- White pepper powder ; ½ tsp.
- Aromat powder ; ½ tsp.
- Honey ; 2-3 tbsp.
- Sesame oil. ; ½ tsp.
- Oil ; To Deep Fry

Spring Onion / coriander leaves as needed for garnish.

METHOD:-

Soak the whole stems in water for 30 minutes. Peel the skin of the lotus stem and slice it in slanting way.

Soak them in water mixed with little salt for 10minutes. Drain the excess water and wipe.

Dust the stems with corn flour + refined flour + salt to form a coating.

Heat oil in a deep frying pan and deep fry on medium flame until it is crispy and golden

Keep aside.

In pan heat oil, add Garlic, Ginger, Onion, Celery, Green chilli, and Thai red chilli stir fry for a min.

Add salt, aromat powder and white pepper powder.

Cook on low flame for few seconds. Once the sauce thickens add the fried stems.

Garnish with chopped spring onions and coriander. Serve hot...

SZECHUAN CORN DUMPLINGS

FOR CORN BALL

Ingredients: Quantity produced: 1 portion

- Sweet corn par boiled   ;   100 grams
- Garlic chopped   ;   1 tsp
- Ginger chopped   ;   1 tsp.
- Green chillies chopped   ;   ½ tsp.
- Red Thai chilli   ;   ½ tsp.
- Coriander chopped   ;   1 tbsp.
- Salt   ;   To taste
- White pepper powder   ;   ½ tsp.
- Aromat powder   ;   ½ tsp.
- Corn flour   ;   1 ½ tbsp.
- Refined flour   ;   1 ½ tsp.
- Chopped celery   ;   1 tbsp.

For Szechuan sauce

- Oil   ;   1 tbsp.
- Garlic chopped   ;   1 tbsp.
- Ginger chopped   ;   1 tbsp
- Celery chopped   ;   1 tbsp.
- Onion chopped   ;   1 ½ tbsp.
- Red & Green chillies chopped ;   1 tbsp.
- Red chilli paste   ;   ½ tsp.
- Tomato ketchup   ;   2 tbsp.
- Salt   ;   To taste
- Aromat powder   ;   ½ tsp.
- White pepper powder   ;   ½ tsp.
- Spring onion chopped   ;   3 strips
- Coriander chopped   ;   For garnish

METHOD:-

In a large bowl take sweet corn, ginger, garlic, green & Thai red chilli coriander, and aromat powder, and corn flour, refined flour and white pepper powder.

Mix well, make sure to mash and combine well forming dough. Divide the dough in equal size and make a smooth ball. Deep fry in hot oil

Fry on medium flame, until the corn ball turn golden brown and crisp.

Keep aside. Heat up a wok and put oil, ginger and garlic Sauté well.

Add Chopped celery, onion, and Thai chilli along with green chillies, Add tomato ketchup, and red chilli paste. Sprinkle salt, aromat powder, white pepper powder, spring onion, coriander, 1cup of water. Mix well,

Cook on medium high flame. Simmer the flame and cook until sauce become medium thick. Add fried corn dumplings, and chopped spring onions. Serve piping hot.

CHILLI JACKFRUIT

INGREDIENTS   Quantity produced: 1portion

- Jackfruit cut &par boiled ; 200grm.
- Refined flour ; 3 tbsp.
- Corn Flour ; 2 tbsp.
- To taste ; Salt
- Garlic chopped ; 2 tbsp.
- Ginger chopped ; 1 tbsp.
- Onion chopped ; 2 tbsp.
- Thai red chilli chopped ; ½ tsp.
- Green chilli chopped ; ½ tsp.
- Tomato Ketchup ; 2 tbsp,
- Chilli paste ; 2 tbsp.
- Soya sauce ; 1 tbsp
- Vinegar ; 1 tbsp.
- Salt ; To taste
- White pepper powder ; ½ tsp.
- Aromat powder ; ½ tsp.
- Spring onion chopped ; 1 tbsp.,
- Coriander chopped ; 1 tbsp,
- Oil ; To Deep Fry

METHOD:-.

In a mixing bowl add kathal, salt, white pepper powder, chilli paste, aromat powder and mix well. Coat the pieces of kathal in the corn flour and deep Fry until turn into nice golden brown colour keep aside.

Heat up a wok and put oil, ginger and garlic, onion, Thai red chilli & green chilli sauté well.

Add tomato ketchup, chilli paste. Sprinkle salt, aromat powder, white pepper powder, spring onion, coriander, 1cup of water& soya sauce, vinegar Mix well; Simmer the flame and cook until sauce becomes medium thick. Add fried kathal and chopped spring onions& coriander. Serve piping hot.

SOUP

VEGETABLE MANCHOW SOUP

Ingredients: Quantity produced: 1 portion

- Carrots chopped   : 1 tbsp.
- Green beans chopped   : 1 tbsp
- Cabbage chopped   : 1 tbsp.
- Mushroom chopped   : 1 tbsp.
- Ginger chopped   : ½ tsp.
- Garlic chopped   : ½ tsp.
- Green chilli chopped   : ½ tsp.
- Coriander chopped   : 1 tbsp.
- Salt   : to taste
- White pepper powder   : a pinch
- Corn flour   : 1 tbsp.
- Vegetable stock   : 1 ½ cup
- Noodles fried   : for garnish

METHOD

In wok add vegetable stock let it come to boil on high flame add ginger, garlic, chili and vegetable after cooking a while season with salt, aromat powder, white pepper powder and simmer for 1 minute. Now add corn flour slurry to thicken. Turn off the flame

Serve piping hot with the fried noodle.

LEMON CORIANDER SOUP

Ingredients: Quantity produced: 1 portion

- Mushroom sliced   ;   10gram.
- Green beans diamond cut   ;   05 gram...
- Broccoli sliced   ;   05 gram.
- Cauliflower sliced   ;   05 gram.
- Carrot sliced   ;   10gram.
- Coriander chopped   ;   1 tbsp.
- Spring onion chopped   ;   1 tbsp.
- Aromat powder   ;   1 pinch
- Salt   ;   to taste
- White pepper powder   ;   a pinch.
- Sesame oil   ;   a few drops.
- Vegetable stock   ;   1 ½ cup
- Lemon juice   ;   ½ tbsp.

METHOD

In wok add vegetable stock let it come to boil on high flame add mushroom, green bean, broccoli, cauliflower, carrot, coriander and spring onion. After cooking a while season with salt, aromat powder, white pepper powder and simmer for 1 minute. Finish with lemon juice and sesame oil Turn off the flame.

Serve piping hot.

HOT 'N' SOUR SOUP

Ingredients: Quantity produced: 1 portion

- Carrots Julian   ;   15gram
- Spinach Julian   ;   2-3 leaf
- Cabbage Julian   ;   15 grams.
- Shitake Mushroom sliced ;   1-2 pcs
- Tofu Julian   ;   10 grams
- Chilli paste   ;   ½ tsp.
- Salt   ;   to taste
- White pepper powder   ;   a pinch
- Corn flour   ;   1 tbsp.
- Vegetable stock   ;   1 ½ cup
- Vinegar   ;   1 tbsp.
- Chilli oil   ;   a few drops
- Aromat powder   ;   ½ tsp.
- Soya sauce   ;   1 tbsp.

METHOD

In wok add vegetable stock let it come to boil on high flame add cabbage, carrot, spinach, shitake mushroom, tofu , chili paste, salt, aromat powder, white pepper powder, vinegar, soya sauce and simmer for 1 minute. Now add corn flour slurry to thicken. Turn off the flame
Serve piping hot.

GARLIC AND SPRING ONION SOUP

Ingredients: Quantity produced: 1 portion

- Carrots chopped : 1 tbsp.
- Green beans chopped : 1 tbsp
- Cabbage chopped : 1 tbsp.
- Garlic chopped : 1 tbsp.
- Green chilli chopped : ½ tsp.
- Coriander chopped : 1 tbsp.
- Spring onion chopped : 1 tbsp.
- Salt : to taste
- Aromat powder : ½ tsp.
- White pepper powder : a pinch
- Corn flour : 1 tbsp.
- Vegetable stock : 1 ½ cup

METHOD

Heat the oil in a pan once hot add garlic. Sauté for a minute then add vegetable stock let it come to boil on high flame add spring onion, vegetables, green chili, coriander after cooking a while season with salt, aromat powder, white pepper powder and simmer for 1 minute. Now add corn flour slurry to thicken. Turn off the flame

Serve piping hot.

SALAD

KIMCHI SALAD

INGRIDENTS   Quantity produced

- Chinese cabbage   ;   80 gram
- Chilli paste   ;   2tbsp
- Tomato ketchup   ;   2tbsp
- Oyster sauce vegetarian ;   2 tsp.
- Salt   ;   to taste
- White pepper   ;   ½ tsp.
- Sesame seed roasted   ;   1tbsp

METHOD;-

Wash and cut cabbage. Soak in salted water 3 hours. Transfer in the strainer for few minutes and squeeze to remove excess water.

Add all of the salad ingredients to a large bowl. Mix it well. And serve sprinkle sesame seeds.

RAW PAPAYA SALAD

INGRIDENTS   Quantity produced

- Carrot Julian   ;   10 gram
- Raw papaya Julian   ;   40gram
- Thai red chilli Julian   ;   1pc
- Green chilli Julian   ;   1pc
- Lemon juice   ;   ½ tsp.
- Jaggery melted   ;   2tbsp
- Tamarind paste   ;   1tbsp
- Sugar   ;   ½ tsp.
- Salt   ;   to taste
- White pepper powder   ;   ½ tsp.
- Peanut crushed   ;   15 gram

METHOD;

Mix jaggery, tamarind, sugar, salt for the dressing in a small bowl and set aside.

In a large bowl, mix the green papaya, carrots, green and red chilli and red chilli and peanuts. Pour in the dressing add lemon juice, white pepper powder and toss to coat the vegetables with the dressing. serve immediately.

CHINESE PICKLE

INGRIDENTS   Quantity produced

- Vinegar   ;   100 ml
- Sugar   ;   100 ML
- Salt   ;   to taste
- Carrot peeled and cut   ;   30gram
- Cucumber peeled cut   ;   30gram
- Capsicum   ;   30gram
- Thai red chilli chopped   :   ½ tsp.
- Green chilli chopped   ;   ½ tsp.

METHOD;-

In bowl combine vinegar, sugar, salt, Thai red chilli and green chilli, stir occasionally until the sugar and salt get dissolved. Pour the liquid over the vegetables. Keep in fridge at least 2 hours.

MAIN COURSE

TOFU IN GINGER SAUCE

Ingredients: Quantity produced: 1 portion

- Tofu   ; 150gram
- Oil   ; 2 tbsp
- Onion chopped   ; 15gram
- Ginger chopped   ; 15gram
- Red & green chili chopped   ; 15gram
- Vegetable stock   ; 1 cup
- Spring onion chopped   ; 10gram
- Coriander chopped   ; 15gram
- Salt   ; to taste
- Aromat powder   ; ½ tsp.
- White pepper powder   ; 1 tbsp.
- Vinegar   ; ½ tbsp.
- Soya sauce   ; 1 tsp.
- Corn flour   ; for thickness
- Chili oil   ; few drops.

METHOD;-

In a bowl add to tofu, soya sauce, salt, aromat powder, white pepper powder & mix.

Then add in enough corn flour to coat tofu so they're almost fully white and mostly dry. Deep fry in hot oil until cooked through and crispy

In a pan add 2 tbsp. of oil; add ginger, onion, red chilli and green chilli. Sauté well.

Then add vegetable stock, salt, aromat powder & white pepper powder, spring onion, coriander, soya sauce and vinegar. Stir for a while, now add corn flour slurry to thicken.

Add in fried crispy tofu and chilli oil, mix thoroughly

Serve in a dish and garnish with spring onion.

MUSHROOM IN HOT CHILLI SAUCE

Ingredients: Quantity produced: 1 portion

- Mushroom par boiled   ;   170 gram
- Oil   ;   2 tbps
- Garlic chopped   ;   15 gram
- Ginger chopped   ;   15 gram
- Onion chopped   ;   15 gram
- Thai red chili chopped   ;   1 tbps
- Vegetable stock   ;   1 ½ cup
- Salt   ;   to taste
- Aromat powder   ;   ½ tbsp.
- Chili paste   ;   1 tbps
- Tomato ketchup   ;   2 tbsp.
- Coriander chopped   ;   1 tbps
- Spring onion   ;   1 tbps
- Corn flour   ;   for thickness
- Chili oil   ;   for garnish

METHOD;-

In a wok heat the oil, add chopped garlic, ginger, onion and Thai red chili cook until a nice aroma comes out.

Then add vegetable stock, salt, aromat powder, white pepper powder, chili paste, tomato ketchup, coriander and spring onion Simmer for 1 minute. Now add corn flour slurry to thicken, add mushroom and finish with chili oil. Garnish with spring onion and serve hot.

SZECHUAN PANEER

- Paneer ; 180 gram
- Corn flour ; enough to coat paneer
- Oil ; 1 tbsp.
- Garlic chopped ; 1 tbsp.
- Ginger chopped ; 1 tbsp
- Celery chopped ; 1 tbsp.
- Onion chopped ; 1 ½ tbsp.
- Red & Green chillies chopped ; 1 tbsp.
- Red chilli paste ; ½ tsp.
- Tomato ketchup ; 2 tbsp.
- Soya sauce ; 1 tbsp
- Vinegar ; 1 tbsp.
- Salt ; To taste
- Aromat powder ; ½ tsp.
- White pepper powder ; ½ tsp.
- Spring onion chopped ; 3 strips
- Coriander chopped ; For garnish

METHOD:-

In a bowl add paneer, salt, white pepper powder, aromat powder, soya sauce & mix. Then add in enough corn flour to coat paneer, so they're almost fully white and mostly dry deep fry in hot oil until cooked through and crispy Keep aside.

Heat up a wok and put oil, ginger, onion, celery, red & green chilli. Sauté well until a nice aroma comes out.

Then add vegetable stock, chili paste, tomato ketchup, soya sauce, vinegar, salt, aromat powder, white pepper powder, coriander and spring onion. Simmer for 1 minute; now add corn flour slurry to thicken. Add fried paneer and stir for a while, garnish with spring onion and coriander. Serve hot

PINEAPPLE IN SPICY SOYA SAUCE

Ingredients: Quantity produced: 1portion

- Pine apple (cut)   ;   180gram
- Garlic chopped   ;   15gram
- Ginger chopped   ;   15gram
- Onion chopped   ;   15 gram
- Thai red chili chopped ;   1tbps
- Green chili chopped   ;   1 tsp
- Vegetable stock   ;   1 ½ cup
- Salt   ;   to taste
- Aromat powder   ;   ½ tbsp.
- White pepper powder   ;   a pinch
- Chili paste   ;   1tbps
- Soya sauce   ;   1tbsp.
- Coriander chopped   ;   1tbps
- Spring onion   ;   1tbps
- Corn flour   ;   enough to coat pineapple
- Chili oil   ;   for garnish
- Oil   ;   for frying

METHOD;-

In a bowl add to pineapple, chilli paste, salt, aromat powder, white pepper powder, soya sauce & mix.

Then add in enough corn flour to coat pineapple so they're almost fully white and mostly dry. Deep fry in hot oil until cooked through and crispy

In a pan add 2 tbsp. of oil; add garlic, onion, ginger, Thai red chilli, and green chilli. Sauté well.

Then add vegetable stock, salt, aromat powder & white pepper powder, chilli paste soya sauce, coriander and spring onion. Simmer for 1 minute. Now add corn flour slurry to thicken add fried pineapple and stir for few seconds.

Serve in a dish and garnished with spring onion.

THREE TREASURES VEGETABLES WITH TOFU

Ingredients: Quantity produced: 1portion

- Broccoli, blanched   ;   45gram
- Bamboo shoot   ;   45gram
- Tofu   ;   45gram
- Shitake mushroom   ;   45 gram
- Oil   ;   2tbsp.
- Garlic chopped   ;   15gram
- Ginger chopped   ;   15gram
- Onion chopped   ;   15gram
- Celery chopped   ;   15gram
- Red & green chili chopped   ;   15gram
- Vegetable stock   ;   1 ½ cup
- Salt   ;   to taste
- Aromat powder   ;   ½ tsp.
- Chili paste   ;   1tbsp
- Tomato ketchup   ;   1tbsp.
- Vinegar   ;   1tbsp
- Coriander chopped   ;   1tbsp
- Spring onion chopped   ;   1tbsp
- Corn flour   ;   3tbsp
- Chili oil   ;   few drops

METHOD;-

In a wok heat the oil, add chopped garlic, ginger celery, onion, green chili and red chili until a nice aroma comes out.

Then add vegetable stock, salt, aromat powder, white pepper powder, chili paste, tomato ketchup, vinegar, coriander and spring onion. Simmer for 1 minute now add corn flour slurry to thicken. Mix all the vegetables and stir for a while. Garnish with spring onion and chilli oil. Serve hot.

CHILLI BASIL CAULIFLOWER

INGRIDENTS   Quantity produced: 1portion

- Cauliflower, par boiled ; 170 gram
- Basil leaves ; 10 -12
- Onion chopped ; 15gram
- Garlic chopped ; 15gram
- Ginger chopped ; 15gram.
- Thai red & green chilli (diamond cut) ; 15gram.
- Vegetable stock ; 1 ½ cup
- Salt ; to taste.
- White Pepper powder ; 1 ½ tsp.
- Chilli paste ; 1tbsp.
- Oyster sauce vegetarian ; 1½ tbsp.
- .Soya sauce ; ½ tbsp.
- Corn flour ; for thickness.
- .Aromat powder ; ½ tbsp.
- Spring onions ; 2tbsp
- Chilli oil ; a few drops.
- Oil ; 2tbsp.

METHOD

In a pan add 2 tbsp. of oil add basil, garlic, ginger, chilli, Thai red chilli and onion. Sauté well.

Then add vegetable stock, salt, aromat powder, white pepper powder, chilli paste, oyster sauce and soya sauce. Simmer for 1 minute; now add corn flour slurry to thicken.

Add in cauliflower and spring onion. mix thoroughly

Serve in a dish and garnish with spring onion.

BABY CORN IN BLACK PEPPER SAUCE

Ingredients:　　　　　　Quantity produced: 1portion

- Baby corn par boiled　;　170gram
- Oil　;　2tbsp
- Garlic chopped　;　15gram
- Onion chopped　;　15gram
- Ginger chopped　;　15gram
- Spring onion chopped　;　10gram
- Coriander chopped　;　10gram
- Salt　;　to taste
- Aromat powder　;　½ tsp.
- Black pepper crushed　;　1 tbsp.
- Vinegar　;　½ tbsp.
- Vegetable stock　;　1 cup
- Corn flour　;　to thicken
- Chili oil　;　few drops
- Sesame oil　;　½ tsp.

METHOD;-

In a wok heat the oil, add chopped garlic, ginger, onion and cook until a nice aroma comes out.

Then add vegetable stock, black pepper, salt, aromat powder, coriander, spring onion and vinegar. Simmer for 1 minute. Now add corn flour slurry to thicken add baby corn and finish with chili oil and sesame oil garnish with spring onion and serve hot.

KACHALU IN TIRYAKI SAUCE

Ingredients:		Quantity produced
• Kachalu blanched	;	180gram
• Salt	;	to taste
• Aromat powder	;	½ tsp.
• White pepper powder	;	½ tsp.
• Soya sauce	;	½ tsp.
• Corn flour	;	enough to coat kachalu
• Jaggery	;	100gram
• Ginger	;	50gram
• Kikkoman soya sauce	;	200ml
• Spring onion chopped	;	15gram

METHOD;-

For teriyaki sauce combine the Kikkoman soya, jaggery, ginger to a small saucepan and simmer for about 4 minutes until thickened. Keep aside.

In a bowl add kachalu, salt, white pepper powder, aromat powder, soya sauce & mix. Then add in enough corn flour to coat kachalu, so they're almost fully white and mostly dry deep fry in hot oil until cooked through and crispy.

In a pan add teriyaki sauce and fried kachalu, cook, stirring often, until combined, serve hot.

CHINESE GREEN IN NOODLE NEST

Ingredients: **Quantity produced: 1portion**

- Broccoli, blanched ; 18gram
- Pock Choy, blanched ; 18gram
- Shitake mushroom, soaked ; 18gram
- White fungus mushroom, soaked ; 18gram
- Black fungus mushroom, soaked ; 18gram
- Asparagus, blanched ; 18gram
- Chinese cabbage, blanched ; 18gram
- Snow peas, blanched ; 18gram
- Zucchini slice, blanched ; 18gram
- Carrot sliced, blanched ; 18gram
- Noodle boiled ; 60gram
- Corn flour ; enough to coat noodle
- Oil ; for frying
- Garlic chopped ; 15 gram
- Oyster sauce vegetarian ; 1tbsp
- Salt ; to taste
- Aromat powder ; ½ tsp.
- Spring onion diamond cut ; 15gram

METHOD:-

For the noodle nest In a bowl add to noodle add in enough corn flour to coat noodle so they're almost fully white and mostly dry. Deep fry in hot oil to help of two tea strainers until cooked through and crispy

In a pan add 2 tbsp. of oil; add garlic, sauté well.

Then add vegetable stock, oyster sauce, salt, aromat powder & white pepper powder, spring onion and stir for a while.

Add all vegetables and mix thoroughly

Serve on a plate in noodle nest and garnish with spring onion.

ZUCCHINI IN ONION GINGER SAUCE

Ingredients: Quantity produced: 1portion

- Zucchini slice blanched   ;   150gram
- Oil   ;   2tbsp
- Green chili chopped   ;   15gram
- Onion chopped   ;   15gram
- Ginger chopped   ;   15gram
- Spring onion chopped   ;   10gram
- Coriander chopped   ;   15gram
- Salt   ;   to taste
- Aromat powder   ;   ½ tsp.
- White pepper powder   ;   1 tbsp.
- Vinegar   ;   ½ tbsp.
- Soya sauce   ;   1tsp.
- Vegetable stock   ;   1 cup
- Corn flour   ;   for thickness
- Chili oil   ;   few drops
- Sesame oil   ;   ½ tsp.

METHOD;-

In a wok heat the oil add chopped onion, ginger, and green chili until a nice aroma comes out.

Then add vegetable stock, salt, aromat powder, white pepper powder coriander and spring onion, simmer for 1 minute. add soya sauce and vinegar. Now add corn flour slurry to thicken, add zucchini and finish with sesame oil for nice flavor, garnish with spring onion and chilli oil serve hot.

EGGPLANT IN OYSTER SAUCE

Ingredients: Quantity produced: 1portion

- Eggplant peeled & cut   ;   180 gram
- .Red chilli paste   ;   1 tsp.
- .Aromat powder   ;   ½ tsp.
- .White pepper powder   ;   ½ tsp.
- Corn flour   ;   Enough to coat soya chaap
- Garlic chopped   ;   1tbsp.
- Green chillies chopped   ;   1 tbsp.
- Spring onion chopped   ;   3 strips
- Vegetable stock   ;   ½ cup
- Soy sauce vegetarian   ;   1 tbsp.
- Red Thai chilli   ;   2-3
- Oyster sauce   ;   1tbps.
- Oil   ;   for deep frying+ 2tbsp.
- Salt   ;   To taste
- Coriander fresh, chopped   ;   For garnish
- Chilli oil   ;   few drops.

METHOD:-

In a bowl add to eggplant, salt, aromat powder, white pepper powder, oyster sauce, soya sauce & mix.

Then add in enough corn flour to coat soya eggplant so they're almost fully white and mostly dry. Deep fry in hot oil until cooked through and crispy

In a pan add 2 tbsp. of oil; add garlic, Thai red chilli, sauté well until a nice aroma comes out.

Then add vegetable stock, oyster sauce, soya sauce, chili paste, salt, aromat powder, coriander and spring onion. Simmer for 1 minute. Now add corn flour slurry to thicken add fried eggplant finish with chili oil garnish with spring onion and serve hot.

POTATO IN HOT GARLIC SAUCE

Ingredients: Quantity produced: 1portion

- Potato par boiled ; 180 gram
- Oil ; for frying
- Garlic chopped ; 15gram
- Onion chopped ; 15gram
- Vegetable stock ; 1 ½ cup
- Salt ; to taste
- Aromat powder ; ½ tsp.
- White pepper powder ; 1/2tsp.
- Tomato ketchup ; 1tbsp.
- Chili paste ; 1tbsp.
- Spring onion chopped ; 15gram
- Coriander chopped ; 15gram
- Corn flour ; 3tbsp
- Vinegar ; 1tbsp.

METHOD:-

In a bowl add to potato, chilli paste, salt, aromat powder, white pepper powder & mix.

Then add in enough corn flour to coat potato so they're almost fully white and mostly dry deep fry in hot oil until cooked through and crispy. In a pan add 2 tbsp. of oil; add garlic, onion sauté well.

Then add vegetable stock, chilli paste, ketchup, salt, aromat powder & white pepper powder, spring onion and coriander and stir for a while. Now add corn flour slurry to thicken.

Add in fried crispy potatoes. Finish with vinegar and mix thoroughly Serve in a dish and garnish with spring onion and coriander.

EXOTIC VEGETABLE IN GARLIC SAUCE

Ingredients: Quantity produced: 1 portion

- Cabbage diced   ;   40gram
- Carrot sliced   ;   5gram
- Zucchini sliced   ;   10gram
- Mushroom sliced   ;   10gram
- Pock Choy cut   ;   10 gram
- Mix bell pepper diced   ;   10gram
- Baby corn diced   ;   10gram
- Garlic chopped   ;   1tbsp
- Onion chopped   ;   2tbsp
- Coriander chopped   ;   1tbsp
- Spring onion chopped   ;   1 tbsp.
- Salt   ;   to taste
- White pepper powder   ;   1/2 tsp.
- Aromat powder   ;   ½ tsp.
- Vinegar   ;   1tbsp.
- Sesame oil   ;   1tbsp
- Corn flour   ;   a few drops
- Oil   ;   2 tbsp.

METHOD;-

In a wok heat the oil add chopped garlic, onion and cook until a nice aroma comes out now add bell pepper, baby corn, carrot, cabbage, zucchini, mushroom, pock choy and stir fry until vegetables are crisp-tender.

Then add vegetable stock, salt, aromat powder, white pepper powder, vinegar, coriander and spring onion. Simmer for 1 minute. Finish with the sesame oil Garnish with spring onion leaves and serve hot.

SOYA CHAAP IN BLACK BEAN SAUCE

Ingredients: Quantity produced: 1portion

- Soya chaap   ;   100gram
- Corn flour   ;   Enough to coat soya chaap
- Ginger chopped   ;   2tbsp
- Garlic chopped   ;   2tbsp
- Onion chopped   ;   2tbsp
- Red Thai chilli chopped ;   ½ tsp.
- Green chilli chopped   ;   ½ tsp.
- Coriander chopped   ;   1tbsp
- Spring onion chopped   ;   1tbsp
- Mix Bell pepper diced   ;   30gram
- Black bean paste   ;   2tbsp
- Chilli paste   ;   1 tbsp.
- Salt   ;   to taste
- Aromat powder   ;   ½ tbsp.
- White pepper powder   ;   ½ tbsp.
- Vinegar   ;   1tbsp
- Dark soya sauce   ;   1tbsp
- Chilli oil   ;   a few drops
- Oil   ;   for frying

METHOD;-

In a bowl add soya chaap with chilli oil, salt, aromat powder, white pepper powder, soya sauce & mix. Then add in enough corn flour to coat soya chaap so they're almost fully white and mostly dry. Deep fry in hot oil until cooked through and crispy keep aside

VEGETABLE BALL IN MANCHURIAN GRAVY

Ingredients: Quantity produced: 1 portion

- Cabbage chopped ; 40gram
- Beans chopped ; 5gram
- Corn boiled ; 5gram
- Carrot chopped ; 5gram
- Cauliflower chopped ; 8gram
- Green chilli chopped ; 1tbsp
- Ginger chopped ; 1tbsp
- Onion chopped ; 2tbsp
- Thai red chilli chopped ; 1tsp
- Coriander chopped ; 1tbsp
- Spring onion chopped ; 1 tbsp.
- Green chilli chopped ; 1tsp
- Salt ; to taste
- White pepper powder ; 1/2 tsp.
- Aromat powder ; ½ tsp.
- Soya sauce ; 1tbsp
- Corn flour ; 3+1tbsp.
- Refined flour ; 3 tbsp.
- Oil ; for frying
- Vegetable stock ; ½ cup
- Chilli paste ; ½ tbsp.
- Vinegar ; ½ tbsp.

METHOD;-

Add cabbage, carrot, bean, corn, cauliflower, green chilli red chilli, and coriander, ginger, salt, aromat powder and white pepper powder to a mixing bowl.

Then add 3 tbsp. corn flour & refined flour Mix well, make sure to mash and combine well. Divide in equal size and make a smooth ball Deep fry in hot oil and keep aside.

To begin making the Manchurian Sauce, Heat Oil in a wok on high heat; add garlic, ginger, onion, red chilli, green chillies and stir-fry for a few seconds.

Then add vegetable stock, salt, aromat powder, white pepper powder, coriander, spring onion, chili paste, soya sauce and vinegar and simmer for 1 minute. Now add corn flour slurry to thicken. Put the fried Vegetable balls in the sauce and stir-fry on high heat for few minutes. Garnish with spring onion leaves and serve hot.

VEGETABLE CHOPSUEY

Ingredients: Quantity produced: 1portion

- Noodle boiled   ;   to serve
- Carrot Julian   ;   20gram
- Cabbage Julian   ;   20gram
- Onion sliced   ;   20gram
- Broccoli sliced   ;   20gram
- Baby corn sliced   ;   20gram
- Bell pepper Julian   ;   20gram
- Pine apple slice   ;   20gram
- Cucumber slice   ;   20gram
- Oil   ;   2tbsp
- Garlic chopped   ;   1tbsp.
- Salt   ;   to taste
- Aromat powder   ;   ½ tbsp.
- White pepper powder ;   ½ tsp.
- Chili paste   ;   1 tsp.
- Tomato ketchup   ;   1tbsp.
- Vinegar.   ;   1 tbsp.
- Corn flour.   ;   3 tbsp.

METHOD;-

First shallow fry noodle and add salt, aromat powder, white pepper powder and keep aside. Heat the oil in a wok once it's hot add garlic, carrot, onion, cabbage, bell pepper, baby corn, broccoli, pine apple, cucumber. Sauté for 1-2 minutes,

Then add vegetable stock, salt, aromat powder, white pepper powder, chili paste, tomato ketchup and vinegar and simmer for 1 minute. Now add corn flour slurry to thicken. Turn off the flame serve over the noodle,

NOODLE

VEGETABLE HAKKA NOODLE

Ingredients: Quantity produced: 1 portion

- Noodles boiled   ;   70 gram.
- Mixed bell pepper   ;   20 gram
- Onion sliced   ;   10 gram
- Carrot Julian   ;   10 gram
- Cabbage shredded   ;   10 gram
- Aromat powder   ;   1 tsp.
- White pepper powder   ;   ½ tsp.
- Soy Sauce   ;   1 tbsp.
- Vinegar   ;   1 tsp.
- Salt   ;   1 tsp.
- Oil   ;   2 tsp.
- Butter   ;   1 tbsp

METHOD

Pour oil and butter to the wok and heat it on a high flame Add onion, bell pepper, carrot and cabbage. Sauté until a nice aroma comes out.

Add the noodle, salt, aromat powder, white pepper powder, vinegar, soya sauce

Toss well and fry for another 2 minutes. Place on a plate garnish with mixed bell pepper. Serve hot.

CHILLI GARLIC NOODLE

Ingredients: Quantity produced: 1 portion

- Noodles boiled   ;   70 gram.
- Mixed bell pepper   ;   20 gram
- Onion sliced   ;   10gram
- Carrot Julian   ;   10 gram
- Cabbage shredded   ;   10gram
- Garlic chopped   ;   1 tbsp.
- Dry red chilli   ;   2pcs
- Aromat powder   ;   01 tsp.
- White pepper powder   ;   ½ tsp.
- Chilli paste   ;   01 tsp.
- Tomato ketchup   ;   01 tbsp.
- Vinegar   ;   01 tsp.
- Salt   ;   01 tsp.
- Oil   ;   2 tsp.
- Butter   ;   2 cubes
- Spring onion   ;   20gram.

METHOD

Pour oil and butter to the wok and heat it on a high flame Add garlic, dry chilli and fry for just 15 seconds then add bell pepper, onion, carrot, cabbage, sauté until a nice aroma comes out.

Add the salt, aromat powder, white pepper powder, chilli paste, tomato ketchup, vinegar and noodle,

Toss well and fry for another 2 minutes. Placed on a plate garnish with mixed bell pepper and spring onion serve hot.

SHANGHAI NOODLE

Ingredients: Quantity produced: 1 portion

- Noodles boiled   ;   70 gram.
- Mixed bell pepper   ;   20 gram
- Onion sliced   ;   10gram
- Carrot Julian   ;   10 gram
- Cabbage shredded   ;   10gram
- Garlic chopped   ;   1 tbsp.
- Ginger chopped   ;   1 tbsp
- Celery chopped   ;   1 tbsp.
- Red & green chilli chopped ; 1tbsp.
- Aromat powder   ;   01 tsp.
- White pepper powder   ;   ½ tsp.
- Chilli paste   ;   01 tsp.
- Tomato ketchup   ;   01 tbsp.
- Salt   ;   01 tsp.
- Oil   ;   2 tsp.
- Butter   ;   1 tbsp.
- Spring onion   ;   10gram.

METHOD

Pour oil and butter to the wok and heat it on a high flame Add garlic, onion, ginger, celery, red& green chilli, bell pepper, carrot, cabbage, sauté until a nice aroma comes out.

Add the chilli paste, tomato ketchup, salt, aromat powder, white pepper powder, spring onion and noodle,

Toss well and fry for another 2 minutes place on a plate garnish with mixed bell pepper and spring onion serve hot.

SINGAPORIAN NOODLE

Ingredients: Quantity produced: 1 portion

- Noodles boiled   ;   70 gram.
- Mixed bell pepper   ;   20 gram
- Onion sliced   ;   10gram
- Carrot Julian   ;   10 gram
- Cabbage shredded   ;   10gram
- Spinach Julian   ;   10 gram.
- Garlic chopped   ;   1 tbsp.
- Aromat powder   ;   01 tsp.
- White pepper powder   ;   ½ tsp.
- Curry powder   ;   1 tbsp.
- Chilli paste   ;   01 tsp.
- Vinegar   ;   01 tsp.
- Salt   ;   01 tsp.
- Oil   ;   2 tsp.
- Butter   ;   1tbsp
- Spring onion   ;   for garnish.

METHOD

Pour oil and butter to the wok and heat it on high flame. Add garlic, bell pepper, onion, carrot, cabbage, spinach sauté until a nice aroma comes out.

Add the curry powder, salt, aromat powder, white pepper powder and noodle tossed well and fries for another 2 minutes placed on a plate garnish with spring onion serve hot.

Take a wok to make the black bean sauce put oil. Once the oil is hot, add garlic, ginger, onion, Thai red chilli, green chilli, and bell pepper sauté well.

Then add the water and simmer for a couple minutes then add black bean paste, chilli paste, salt, aromat powder and white pepper powder, coriander, spring onion, vinegar and dark soya sauce and simmer for 1 minute.

Now add corn flour slurry to thicken. Add fried soya chaap and finish with chilli oil and spring onion to let flavours combine. Arrange on a serving plate, serve piping hot.

RICE

VEGETABLE FRIED RICE

Ingredients: Quantity produced: 1 portion

- Rice cooked & cooled ; 170 gram
- Oil ; 1 tbsp.
- Butter ; 1 tbsp.
- Carrots chopped ; 50 gram
- Beans chopped ; 50 gram
- Salt ; to taste
- Aromat powder ; 1 tsp.
- Vinegar ; 1 tsp.
- Spring onion ; 2 tsp.

METHOD

Heat a wok or a large skillet over high heat until very hot. Add 1 tablespoon of oil, butter and then stir continously until the vegetables are crisp-tender.

Then add the rice, aromat powder, white pepper powder, vinegar and spring onion.

Cook, stirring often, until everything is combined and hot and the vegetables are just tender. And adjust the seasonings with salt and white pepper powder,.

Sprinkle the spring onion over the top, and serve.

PINEAPPLE FRIED RICE

Ingredients: Quantity produced: 1 portion

- Rice cooked & cooled   ;   170 gram
- Pineapple dice   ;   50 gram.
- Oil   ;   1 tbsp.
- Butter   ;   1 tbsp.
- Garlic chopped   ;   1 tbsp.
- Onion chopped   ;   1 tbsp.
- Salt   ;   To taste
- Aromat powder   ;   1 tsp.
- . White pepper powder   ;   ½ tsp.
- Spring onion   ;   1 tsp.
- Vinegar   ;   1 tbsp.
- Soya sauce light   ;   1 tsp.
-

METHOD

Heat a wok or a large skillet over high heat until very hot. Add 1 tablespoon of oil, butter then garlic, onion, pineapple then stir for few seconds. Add rice, salt, aromat powder, white pepper powder, spring onion, and vinegar & soya sauce

Cook, stirring often, until everything is combined and hot adjust the seasoning with salt and white pepper powder,

Sprinkle the spring onion, and serve hot.

CORN FRIED RICE

Ingredients:　　　　　　　　Quantity produced: 1 portion

- Rice cooked & cooled　；　170 gram
- Corn boiled　；　50 gram.
- Oil　；　1 tbsp.
- Butter　；　1 tbsp.
- Garlic chopped　；　1tbsp.
- Ginger chopped　；　1tbsp.
- Salt　；　To taste
- Aromat powder　；　1 tsp.
- Spring onion　；　2 tsp.
- White pepper powder　；　½ tsp.
- Vinegar　；　1tbsp.
- Soya sauce　；　1tsp.

METHOD

Heat a wok or a large skillet over high heat until very hot. Add 1 tablespoon of oil, butter then add ginger, garlic, corn. Stir for few seconds add rice, salt, aromat powder, white pepper powder, spring onion, and vinegar & soya sauce

Cook, stirring often, until everything is combined and hot adjust the seasoning with salt and white pepper powder,

Sprinkle the spring onion, and serve hot.

BURNT GARLIC RICE

Ingredients: **Quantity produced: 1 portion**

- Rice cooked & cooled   ;   170 gram
- Oil   ;   1 tbsp.
- Butter   ;   1 tbsp.
- Garlic chopped   ;   1 tbsp.
- Crispy garlic chips   ;   5-6 clove
- Salt   ;   To taste
- Aromat powder   ;   1 tsp.
- Spring onion   ;   2 tsp.
- White pepper powder   ;   ½ tsp.

METHOD

Heat a wok or a large skillet over high heat until very hot. Add 1 tablespoon of oil, butter, chopped garlic to crisp up then add rice, salt, aromat powder, white pepper powder, spring onion.

Cook, stirring often, until everything is combined and hot adjust the seasoning with salt and white pepper powder,.

Sprinkle the crispy garlic, spring onion, and serve hot.

DESSERT

DATE PAN CAKE

INGRIDENTS | | Quantity produced
- Dates chopped ; 6pcs
- Sesame seed roasted ; 5gram
- Spring roll sheet ; 2 no
- Oil ; for frying

METHOD;-

Mixed dates and sesame seed in a bowl and made it like dough then spread in a ball on butter pepper, after that placed it on spring roll sheet. Covered it with another sheet, then cut the remaining from the side. Deep fry in oil till golden and crisp, served with vanilla ice cream.

FRUIT ROLL

INGRIDENTS   Quantity produced

- Mixed fruit chopped   ;   100gram
- Honey   ;   2tsp
- Sesame seed   ;   5gram
- Sugar   ;   1tbsp
- Oil   ;   for frying
- Spring roll sheet   ;   2no

METHOD;-

Add honey to the pan and cook a little, then add sesame seed and then add fruit. Cook for a while then add sugar and stir. After it is ready, leave it to cool for 5 minutes. Then make fruit roll with spring roll sheet & Deep fry in oil till golden and crisp. Served hot with drizzle of honey with cinnamon ice cream / vanilla ice cream.

HONEY FRIED NOODLE

INGRIDENTS   Quantity produced

- Flat noodle   ;   30gram
- Sesame seed roasted   ;   2 tsp.
- .Honey   ;   2 tbsp.
- Vanilla ice cream   ;   1 scoop
- Oil   ;   for frying

METHOD

Deep fry flat noodle in oil till golden and crisp, add honey to the pan and cook a little, then add sesame seed and then add fried noodles and stir.

Serve with the vanilla ice cream.

FRIED ICE CREAM

INGRIDENTS   Quantity produced

- vanilla ice cream scoop   ;   100gm
- Bread crumb   ;   for coating
- Chocolate syrup   ;   1 tbsp.
- Oil   ;   for frying

METHOD

Roll the frozen ice cream balls in the bread crumb two times. Press the mixture firmly onto the ball to create a thick coating. Deep-fry until golden brown, about 10 to 15 seconds. Serve the fried ice cream immediately with chocolate sauce.

www.ingramcontent.com/pod-product-compliance
Lightning Source LLC
LaVergne TN
LVHW061630070526
838199LV00071B/6634